RODEO ROPING

RODEO

Tex McLeese

The Rourke Press, Inc.
Vero Beach, Florida 32964

© 2001 The Rourke Press, Inc.

All rights reserved. No part of this book may be reproduced or utilized in any form or by any means, electronic or mechanical including photocopying, recording, or by any information storage and retrieval system without permission in writing from the publisher.

PHOTO CREDITS:
© Dennis K. Clark: title page, pages 7, 10, 12, 13, 15, 17; © Texas Department of Tourism: cover, pages 8, 18; © Texas Highways Magazine: page 4; Pro Rodeo Cowboy Association: page 21

EDITORIAL SERVICES:
Pamela Schroeder

Library of Congress Cataloging-in-Publication Data

McLeese, Tex, 1950-
   Rodeo roping / Tex McLeese.
      p. cm. — (Rodeo discovery library)
   Includes index.
   Summary: Surveys and describes the three main roping events in rodeo: calf roping, steer roping, and team roping.
   ISBN 1-57103-348-3
   1. Calf roping—United States—Juvenile literature. 2. Steer roping—United States—Juvenile literature. 3. Team roping—United States— Juvenile literature.
[1. Calf roping. 2. Steer roping. 3. Team roping. 4. Rodeos.] I. Title.

GV1834.45.C34 M34 2000
791.8'4—dc21
                                                      00-022994

Printed in the USA

TABLE OF CONTENTS

Rodeo Roping	5
Roping Events	6
Calf Roping	9
Catching the Calf	14
Tying the Calf	16
Judging the Event	19
Team Roping	20
Steer Roping	22
Glossary	23
Index	24

RODEO ROPING

In **rodeo** (ROW dee oh), cowboys use a lot of skills from the Old West of the 1800s. One of those skills was **roping** (ROH ping). On ranches, cowboys roped calves or **steer** (STEAR) to take them out of the herd. Often these were sick animals that needed help. During the early days of the rodeo, cowboys from different ranches would see who could rope and tie an animal the fastest. Roping events are still very popular at every rodeo.

Rodeo rider Bill Dunlap.

ROPING EVENTS

The three main roping events are **calf** (CAF) roping, steer roping, and team roping. In each event cowboys on horses try to rope and tie an animal as fast as they can. Calves are easier to rope. Steer have horns and can weigh 500 pounds or more. Calves are only half that size.

The roper is ready.

CALF ROPING

In calf roping, the cowboy rides his horse and chases after a running calf. He must rope it and tie it as fast as he can. The calf runs as fast as it can to get away. A fast horse that works well with the cowboy is important to winning a calf roping event.

The cowboy chases the running calf.

In calf roping the cowboy and his horse start by backing into the roping box. When they are ready, the cowboy nods his head. The calf gets a head start. The head start is called a "**score**" (SKOR). The score can be anywhere from 5 to 30 feet long. Large rodeos have longer scores.

The calf roper makes his catch.

The roper makes the "head catch."

He quickly ties the calf.

CATCHING THE CALF

When the calf gets to the end of its "score," the cowboy and horse start chasing it. When they get close to the calf, the cowboy swings a loop of rope around and around over his head. This loop of rope is called a "**lasso**" (LASS oh). The other end of the rope is tied to the cowboy's saddle. The cowboy can throw the lasso over any part of the calf. Most of the time cowboys lasso the calf over its head. This is called a "**head catch**" (HED KACH).

The cowboy holds pigging string in his teeth.

TYING THE CALF

After the cowboy ropes the calf, he jumps off his horse and runs to the calf. He grabs the calf by the side of its legs and throws it to the ground. This is called "**flanking**" (FLAN king) the calf. The cowboy has some string in his teeth called "**pigging string**" (PIGG ing STRING). He uses the pigging string to tie three of the calf's legs together. This way the calf can't get up and run away.

The cowboy is done when he throws up his hands.

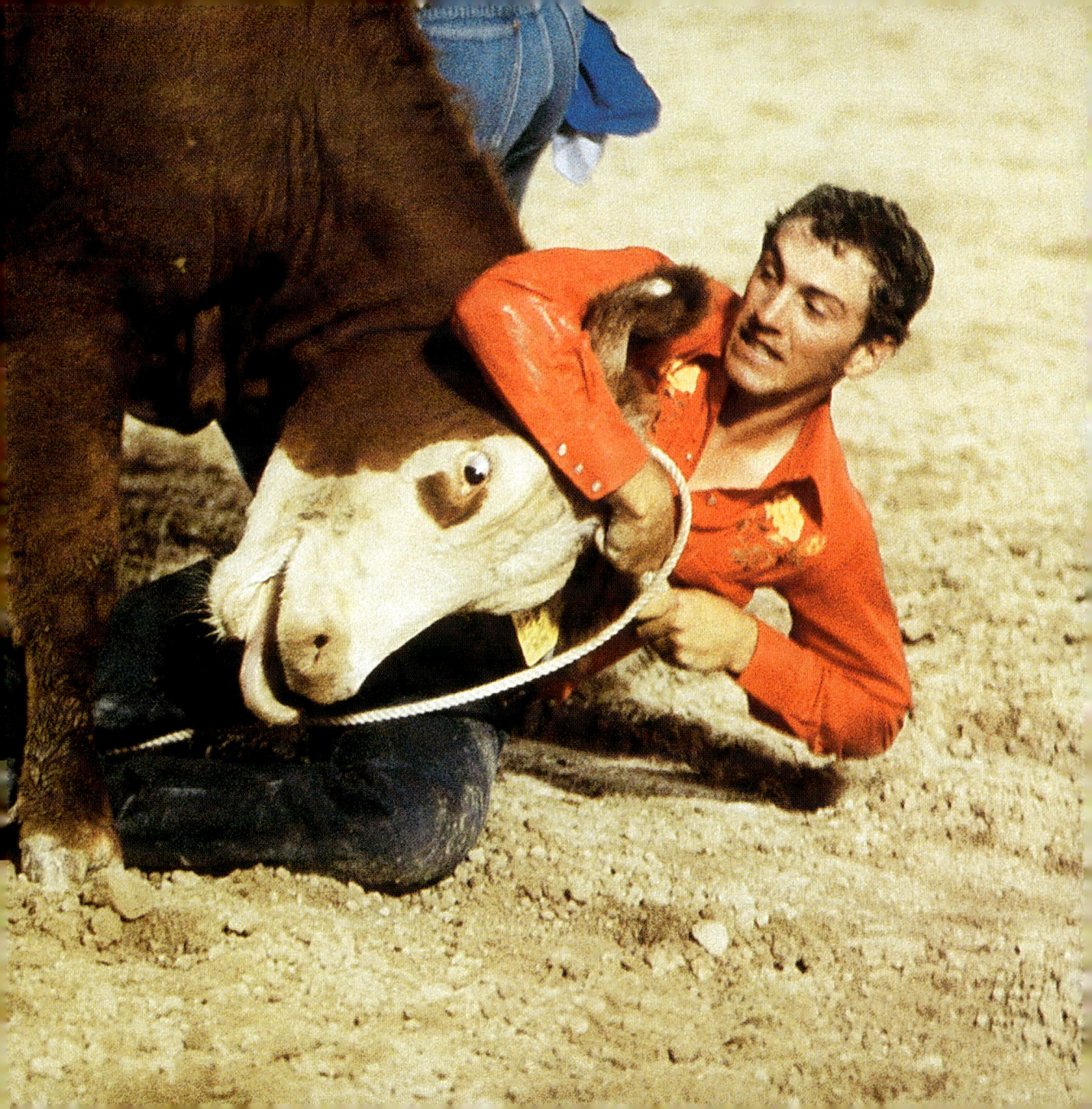

JUDGING THE EVENT

When the cowboy finishes tying the calf, he throws his hands in the air. This is a signal. Now the judge knows the cowboy is done. Most of the time it takes a cowboy less than 10 seconds to rope and tie a calf. The winner is the cowboy that ties the calf the fastest. If the calf kicks free of the rope in 6 seconds or less, the cowboy's turn doesn't count.

The roper gets his steer.

TEAM ROPING

In team roping, two cowboys try to rope and tie a steer. The fastest team is the winner. Each team has a "**header**" (HED ur) and a "**heeler**" (HEE lur). The header is the first rider out of the roper's box. He must lasso the steer's horns. Then the heeler tries to rope both of the steer's back legs. The judge adds 5 seconds to the team's time if the heeler ropes only one leg. The clock stops when the header and heeler pull their ropes tight and face each other. The winning time is often less than 5 seconds.

The header lassos the horns.
The heeler ropes the legs.

STEER ROPING

Most of the time a rodeo will have steer roping or team roping, but not both. In steer roping, it is only legal for the cowboy to rope the animal around the horns. That's to make steer roping different from calf roping. Steer roping is one of the oldest rodeo events. Now it is only held at the largest rodeos. Calf roping and team roping are much more common.

GLOSSARY

calf (CAF) — a young cow or bull

flanking (FLAN king) — grabbing a calf by the side of its legs and throwing it to the ground

head catch (HED KACH) — lassoing a calf over its head

header (HED ur) — team roper who lassos the steer's horns

heeler (HEE lur) — team roper who ropes the steer's back legs

lasso (LASS oh) — a long rope with a loop at the end

pigging string (PIGG ing STRING) — string that the cowboy carries in his teeth to tie the calf's legs together

rodeo (ROW dee oh) — a sport with events using the roping and riding skills that cowboys needed in the Old West

roping (ROH ping) — catching an animal with a rope

score (SKOR) — head start for the calf before the roper starts chasing

steer (STEAR) — a young ox

INDEX

calf roping   6, 9, 11, 22
flanking   16
head catch   14
header   20
heeler   20
judge   19, 20
lasso   14, 20
roping events   6
score   11, 14
steer roping   6, 22
team roping   6, 20, 22
tying   16, 19